*Cyril of Alexandria's Ontological Priority of
Personhood Against Monarchianism*

Cyril of Alexandria's Ontological Priority of Personhood Against Monarchianism

Sherif Mourad

AGORA
UNIVERSITY
PRESS

Cyril of Alexandria's Ontological Priority of Personhood Against Monarchianism

Copyright © 2021 by Agora University Press

All rights reserved. Printed in the United States of America. No part of this book may be used or reproduced in any manner whatsoever without written permission except in the case of brief quotations embodied in critical articles or reviews.

For information contact: aupress@agora.ac
Agora University Press: aupress.org

ISBN 978-1-950831-17-3
Printed in the United States of America

HIS HOLINESS POPE TAWADROS II
118th Pope and Patriarch of the great city of Alexandria and the See of St. Mark

HIS HOLINESS PATRIARCH IGNATIUS APHREM II
Patriarch of Antioch and All the East

Table of Contents

Acknowledgments...vii

Foreword...5

Introduction..11

Terminology...14

The Doctrine of the Holy Trinity: A Spectrum...........20

Cyril's Ontological Priority of Personhood...............41

Personhood Against Monarchianism in Modern Theological Dialogue..59

Further Implications..68

Bibliography... 79

About the Author... 86

Acknowledgements

This book was based on my master's thesis, which in turn originated from an idea that occupied my thoughts for more than 15 years. First, I would like to express my gratitude to Dr. Emmanuel Gergis, who supervised my master's thesis, for his guidance and encouragement, and more importantly, for being my mentor over the past three years. Also, I would like to thank all the faculty members at Holy Transfiguration College for their support.

Ultimately, I give all the glory to the Holy Trinity who gave me the grace to accomplish this work.

Foreword

Crowded discussions on Trinitarian theology in today's academic sphere makes it difficult to advance theological vision based on concrete theological definitions rooted in early Christian sources. As I often advocate, building constructive theology upon a historical vacuum is a risky endeavor. Some contemporary discussions have departed from the realm of theology and have been reduced into empty philosophical equations devoid of the historical and divine dimensions. In short, they are discussions that are keen on keeping the form as a means for declaring intellectual superiority, but unfortunately ignoring the essence which is profoundly necessary for effective renewal of the heart. Consequently, in today's context, less attention is given to the significance and real value of personhood as rooted in a Trinitarian understanding. This theological crisis reflects also on our daily life as we are now facing a real crisis in which the foundational point of reference for humanity, having being created in the image and likeness of a Trinitarian God, has been disfigured. This disfiguration of personhood is happening due to the rise in diluting persons into mere individuals. It is evident that our society has devised a new definition for personhood which is based on purely economic and consumerist key performance indicators and not the Trinitarian-based priority of personhood.

In response to this theological and social crisis, this perceptive study by Sherif Mourad presents us with a fresh outlook for the restoration of the value of personhood and the significance of a person-based priority of being. Sherif was able to masterfully capture this personhood-based ontological priority in Cyril of Alexandria's theology and then he thoughtfully engaged it in a lively discussion with Torrancean and Zizioulan Trinitarian debates. I believe that this work does not only restore and highlight the genuine Alexandrian understanding of personhood, but also helps us understand the necessity for re-evaluating our own humanity in light of this profound definition. I am honored to introduce this important work by Sherif Mourad whose astute thesis research at Agora University has blossomed into this valuable book. I hope that you will find his insights inspiring to elevate our modern discussions both theologically and socially to help restore our view of our Trinitarian God and our own humanity, having been created in His image and likeness.

Emmanuel Gergis, Ph.D.

Associate Professor of Dogmatics
& Systematic Theology
Agora University
April 8, 2021

Introduction

God is, evidently, the nucleus of any theological work, be it scholastic studies or a simple sermon in a small chapel. But the conundrum that persistently confronts theology is that when God is spoken of, He is introduced anonymously most of the time. Perhaps it is more convenient sometimes to speak about God than to define with certainty *who* God is. One can, with insignificant effort, recount God's attributes and benevolences only insofar as it is possible to express His revelation to us. The challenge begins when the task turns out to be the identification of God, indicating precisely *who He is*. Trinitarian theology, being the appropriate discipline of studying the persons of the Holy Trinity and their relation, currently faces an unprecedented challenge. The puzzle at hand is that if every religion has its own god, the question then becomes who is the god that Christianity declares.

Aristotelian philosophy is the foundation of Western civilization. It whittles every facet of modern life. Ultimately, peripatetic thinking has seeped into theology and doctrine, not only in the West, but later in the East as well. The most prominent facet of this is abstract concepts and deductions, manifested in the study of the essence. Contrastively, the Church fathers always taught that God is unknowable in His essence. On the other hand, the Divine revelation of the Holy Trinity is how God intended to make Himself knowable to His creation. Speaking of essence addresses what is common, while the persons, contrarily, identify what is particular. Add to this the other major peril, that is threatening the existence of pure Trinitarian theology: probing the essence apart from the persons. The notion of the *one* essence proves to be very seductive for a substantial number of theologians. The one essence is perceived as the source of the *oneness* of the Trinity. Essence, most of the time, takes center stage, while *persons* are abandoned. According to this epitome, studying the doctrine of God starts to take a monarchic monotheistic approach. "God is one" is regarded as denoting a numeric significance. Consequently, "God is one" no longer speaks of *unity*, a unity in diversity, but rather of singularity. This research resorts to Patristic understanding in an endeavor to resolve the modern theological dilemma of the ontological question. This research seeks to answer the following imperative question: how can the ontological priority of personhood in the theology of Cyril of Alexandria, as opposed to essence, help us respond to the demotion of Trinitarian theology and the dominance of monarchian theology, and its implications, in the modern dialogue between John Zizioulas and Torrancean theology?

    This work begins by illustrating the most relevant terminology of this topic. It then reviews the different perspectives of the doctrine of God in the ancient catholic Church, its most famous controversies, and in modern theology. The following section discusses Cyril's ontological priority of personhood through his Christology and Trinitarian theology. Afterward, the ontological priority of personhood is contrasted against monarchianism in the modern theological dialogue. Finally, the implications of these findings are discussed.

Terminology

Nature (Physis)

In the field of theology oftentimes the term nature is understood to mean essence or substance, i.e., the commonly shared attributes of a certain subset. This meaning is derived from Aristotelian philosophy. This is also how the fathers of the Greek Antiochene line understood *physis*.[1] Of course, the patristic use of the term is in variation.

Clement of Alexandria in the second century defined it as "φύσις ἐστὶν ἡ τῶν πραγμάτων ἀλήθεια."[2] *Physis* is related in meaning to "the truth about something" or "the reality of something." *Physis*, thus, as "reality" is understood as the true identity of a subject within the process of knowledge.[3] According to Torrance, Athanasius applied the term *physis* in the sense of reality or truth.[4]

---

[1] Thomas F. Torrance, *Divine Meaning: Studies in Patristic Hermeneutics* (London: T&T Clark, 1995), 212.

[2] Emmanuel Gergis, "T. F. Torrance and the Christological Realism of the Coptic Orthodox Church of Alexandria" in *T. F. Torrance and Eastern Orthodoxy: Theology in Reconciliation*, Matthew Baker, ed. (Eugene: Wipf and Stock Publishers, 2015), 275.

[3] Thomas F. Torrance, *Theological and Natural Science* (Eugene: Wipf and Stock, 2005), 100.

[4] Gergis, Ibid., 274.

Ousia

Athanasius used the term οὐσία as a synonym to *alethia* and *physis*, meaning "reality."[5] Another use of *ousia* is as a synonym to substance (secondary substance in Aristotelian philosophy or essence) or a primary substance (a subject), signifying "a certain 'this' (τόδε τι)."[6] The term *ousia*, and by extension the term ὁμοούσιος, has its scriptural foundation in Exodus 3:14, according to Cyril of Alexandria, as "I am he who is (Ἐγώ εἰμι ὁ ὤν)" (*LXX*).[7] For the patriarch, it is indicative of the substance. The substance of God, in Cyril's view, though unfathomable stands for a specific shared reality (πρᾶγμᾰ) in God.[8] This is in contrast to the *hypostasis* which refers to what is specific. But when Cyril confronted his opponents, who utilize Aristotelian logic, he employed *ousia* as a "secondary substance" or essence, especially in the Trinitarian context.[9] In special cases as in conjunction with *hypostasis*, Cyril employs *ousia* as primary substance.[10] This is apparent in his discussion of the Nicene Creed. Loon emphasizes that substance for Cyril is more of a "common reality" than a "common universal."[11]

---

[5] Torrance, *Divine Meaning*, 211.
[6] Hans van Loon, *The Dyophysite Christology of Cyril of Alexandria* (Leiden: Brill, 2009), 73.
[7] Ibid., 124.
[8] Ibid., 126.
[9] Ibid., 127.
[10] Ibid., 129.
[11] Ibid., 130.

Hypostasis

The term Hypostasis may refer to substance (*ousia*), as in "from the substance of the Father."[12] This usage is confirmed through the modification that occurred in the Creed of Faith in Constantinople (381), where the phrase "from the essence of the Father" was rendered as "from the Father." Origen tailored the usage of the term to indicate the distinctions of the Trinitarian persons.[13] *Hypostasis* is oftentimes a synonym to *prosopon* in Cyril's writings, where "in his own language the term denotes a 'person,' a rational being, capable of communication with other such beings, capable of a personal relation."[14] A person is a coherent unity in regard to the outside world, taking into account that Cyril is mostly uninterested in the person's composition.[15] This could mean that, for Cyril, the person is irreducible. Accordingly, *hypostasis* may be used as a synonym to *prosopon*. Eventually, the *hypostasis/prosopon* points to a subject; an identity.[16] Cyril of Alexandria implemented the term in his profound Christology and

---

[12] Ibid., 129.
[13] *An Introductory Dictionary of Theology and Religious Studies*, Orlando Espin, James B. Nickoloff, eds. (Collegeville: Liturgical Press, 2007), 597.
[14] van Loon, *The Dyophysite Christology of Cyril of Alexandria*, 509.
[15] Ibid.
[16] *The Theology of St. Cyril of Alexandria: A Critical Appreciation*, Thomas Weinandy and Daniel A. Keating, eds. (London: T&T Clark, 2003), 45.

consequently, developed the notion of hypostatic union to explicate the manner through which the Incarnation ensued.

Hypostatic Union

This term denotes that the union taking place is effected within the hypostasis. The union between the Divine person (the Word) and the human essence is "according to the person" (καθ' ὑπόστασιν).[17] This meaning can be seen in Cyril's statement in *Against Nestorius*: "we affirm this: that the Word personally (according to the person) united to himself flesh."[18] Eventually, this is not a union between two essences, but rather it is an *act* of the person of the Logos acquiring human flesh.[19] This notion was later approved by the Council of Chalcedon of 451 AD.[20]

Perichoresis

It is from *peri* meaning "around" and *chorein* meaning to "advance" or "make room for" in Greek.[21] It may refer to "penetration" where it is equivalent to the Latin term *circumincessio*.[22] In Trinitarian theology, the term

---

[17] Ibid., 41.
[18] Ibid.
[19] Ibid.
[20] *An Introductory Dictionary of Theology and Religious Studies*, Ibid., 598.
[21] James A. Fowler, *Theo-Unity* (Fallbrook: Christ in You Publishing, 2008), 23.
[22] *An Introductory Dictionary of Theology and Religious Studies*, Ibid., 1027.

indicates the three persons' "interpenetration" of one another.²³ Boff suggests that the term's first usage in this manner was by Pseudo-Cyril in the sixth century, and he presents an explanation of its Trinitarian significance.²⁴ First, it has a passive connotation, where one person is dwelling in the others, surrounding the others from all sides, and occupying the same space as the others.²⁵ The second meaning is active and denotes the "interweaving" of one person into the others and with the others.²⁶

Ontology

Its base is Ὄντως (Strong's Number: 3689) which means "being," "real," "true," or "that which is." Ontology is the study of the "being." Where the ontological question searches for answering what is the "cause and purpose of the existential fact."²⁷ Ultimately, *the Being* is the one who possesses an autonomous existence.

Conclusion

Terminology plays a crucial role in inferring a particular meaning. Nevertheless, according to the writer/reader's tradition and worldview, the meaning of the

---

[23] Leonardo Boff, *Trinity and Society*, (Eugene: Wipf and Stock), 135.
[24] Ibid.
[25] Ibid., 136.
[26] Ibid.
[27] Christos Yannaras, *Relational Ontology*, Norman Russell, ed. (Brookline: Holy Cross Orthodox Press, 2011), 4.

terminology used becomes variable. Studying the history of a term's usage is indispensable. It is astonishing how certain terms may at times be synonymous and at other times acquire a completely different meaning. The term *physis* can generally be taken to mean "what something" is or "the definitive reality of something." The term *ousia* is generally understood as the essence or substance. *Hypostasis* is taken as a synonym to person and prosopon. The *hypostatic* union is used to describe the way by which the Incarnation was achieved, i.e. the Son of God *hypostatically* united himself to human nature. *Perichoresis* is the peculiar communal mode of the Trinity's existence, where the persons are interpenetrating each other and dwelling in each other. Cyril of Alexandria was mainly occupied with the underlying conception of a term rather than its superficial meaning.[28] Therefore it is not sufficient to use terminology without it being accompanied by some sort of explication, in addition to recognizing its context. Words should be studied within a collective body of thought in order to acquire a genuine understanding of the ideas they convey. This seems to be one of Cyril's aims in writing his *Thesaurus*.

---

[28] van Loon, *The Dyophysite Christology of Cyril of Alexandria*, 395.

The Doctrine of the Holy Trinity: A Spectrum

The Development of Trinitarian Theology in the Ancient Catholic Church

Justin Martyr

Justin Martyr was born in Samaria around 105.[29] Early on, the apologist inaugurated the discussion about the Son's consubstantiality with the Father,[30] using the analogy of the sun and its rays; both are inseparable. The Father begets the Son from His essence, but not through "abscission," for they are of the same essence.[31] From Gerald L. Bray's compilation of the Church fathers' theology, Justin's thoughts on the Trinity can be summarized as follows: "the Trinity is the one true God [...] the Father is not identical to the Son [...] we know God in a Trinity of persons."[32] In his *Dialogue with Trypho*, Justin describes the Father as non-movable,[33]

---

[29] Justin Martyr, *The Sacred Writings of Justin Martyr,* Marcus Dods, trans. (Alternmünster: Jazzybee Verlag, 2012), 12.

[30] Roger E. Olson and Christopher Alan Hall, *The Trinity* (Grand Rapids: Wm. B. Eerdmans Publishing, 2002), 22.

[31] Justin Martyr, Ibid., 210.

[32] *We Believe in One God: Ancient Christian Doctrine Series, Volume 1,* Gerald L. Bray and Thomas C. Oden, eds. (Downers Grove: IVP Academic, 2009), 63.

[33] This is not to be confused with the Aristotelian understanding; that God is not in interaction with his creation. Rather here Justin Martyr is explicating God's transcendence to the pagan world, and this is to be complemented with his theology of the Logos, through Whom God is

ineffable, and eternal.[34] Also, the Father is not "identical" to His Son, but at the same time, the Son is God.[35]

Theophilus of Antioch

Theophilus is the seventh bishop of Antioch, thought to have died between 185-191 AD.[36] He was the first writer to use the term "triad" theologically.[37] The Trinity is the Father, His Logos, and His Sophia. Later on, Tertullian will adopt Theophilus' term translating it to *Trinitas*.[38]

Origen

Born in 185 AD, Origen was the head of Alexandria's famous Catechetical School from 203-231 AD, and his most significant work on the Trinity was *On First Principles*.[39] Origen was the first "mainstream" author to use the term *homoousios* in a Trinitarian context.[40] The distinction

---

actively working in creation. Thus, God is not contained within Himself but is actually flowing outside of Himself because of his constant movement towards His creation.

[34] *We Believe in One God*, Ibid., 65.

[35] Ibid., 67.

[36] *The Faith of the Early Fathers: Pre-Nicene and Nicene Eras*, William A. Jurgens, trans. (Collegeville: Liturgical Press, 1978), 73.

[37] Rick Rogers, *Theophilus of Antioch: The Life and Thought of a Second-Century Bishop* (Lanham: Lexington Books, 2000), 75.

[38] Marian Hillar, *From Logos to Trinity: The Evolution of Religious Beliefs from Pythagoras to Tertullian* (Cambridge: Cambridge University Press, 2012), 243.

[39] William J. La Due, *The Trinity Guide to the Trinity*, (London: Bloomsbury Academic, 2003), 37.

[40] Tarmo Toom, *Classical Trinitarian Theology: A Textbook* (London: T&T Clark, 2007), 68.

between *ousia* and *hypostasis*—both were generally used, in connection to *physis*, to point to a certain reality—was not that clear in Origen's theology, the work that was later fulfilled in Nicaea by Athanasius.[41] Origen thought of the generation of the Son to be from the Father's will and not from His being.[42] Some scholars tend to accuse Origen of being an advocate of subordinationism. Nevertheless, Ramelli negates this accusation, explicating that Origen's interpretation of 1 Cor. 15:26-28 does not show features of subordination.[43] In fact, Gregory of Nyssa depended on Origen's interpretation to disprove Neo-Arians.[44] Ramelli ingeniously illustrates how Origen's "Trinitarian heritage is found, not in Arianism, but in Nyssen, Athanasius, Eusebius, and the Nicene-Constantinopolitan line."[45]

---

[41] Walter Kasper, *Jesus the Christ: New Edition* (London: T&T Clark, 2011), 229.

[42] Thomas F. Torrance, *Trinitarian Faith: The Evangelical Theology of the Ancient Catholic Faith*, Edition Unstated edition (London: Continuum International Publishing 2003), 85.

[43] Ilaria Ramelli, *The Christian Doctrine of Apokatastasis: A Critical Assessment from the New Testament to Eriugena* (Leiden: Brill, 2013), 588.

[44] Ibid., 375.

[45] Ilaria Ramelli, "Origen's Anti-Subordinationism and Its Heritage in the Nicene and Cappadocian Line," *Vigiliae Christianae* 65, no. 1 (January 1, 2011): 21.

Tertullian

An African as Jerome calls him,[46] who is thought to have died 240.[47] Tertullian is considered to be the first to use pure Trinitarian terminology in his doctrine. In his treatise *Against Praxeas*, Tertullian inaugurated the Church's quest for fighting modalism.[48] The problem with *Praxeas* was that he demoted the ontological triunity of God.[49] As for Tertullian, he argued that God's eternal existence was accompanied by His Reason (*ratio*) and Wisdom (*sophia*).[50] Moltmann lists the most important features of Tertullian's doctrine. These are namely the coining of the term *trinitas*, "Trinitarian differentiation of the *monas*," and "the distinctions in the unity."[51] Consequently, the "One God is not a numerical One," but rather One refers to unity.[52]

Still, in seeking to designate the source of unity within the Divine, Tertullian attributed the monarchy to the Father.[53] For He, the Father, contains all the Divine essence,

---

[46] Ronald D. Burris, *Where Is the Church?: Martyrdom, Persecution, and Baptism in North Africa from the Second to the Fifth Century* (Eugene: Wipf and Stock Publishers, 2012), 24.
[47] Tertullian, *The Writings of Tertullian, Volume II Revised* (Lulu.com, n.d.), 78.
[48] Roger E. Olson, *The Story of Christian Theology: Twenty Centuries of Tradition Reform* (Downers Grove: IVP Academic 1999), 92.
[49] Ibid.
[50] Jurgen Moltmann, *The Trinity and the Kingdom*, (Minneapolis: Fortress Press, 1993), 137.
[51] Ibid., 138.
[52] Ibid., 137.
[53] Ibid., 138.

and the Son and the Spirit are emanations of Him.[54] This reveals that within Tertullian's doctrine of God, unity is not ontologically based, but only ontologically expressed. The one essence is what secures unity.

Athanasius of Alexandria

Driven by soteriological concerns, the 20th Pope of Alexandria sought to demonstrate the Son's consubstantiality with the Father. Athanasius emphasized: If Christ is not truly a God, then "what is at stake is [...] people's salvation."[55] The Son is of the Father's essence, with the only difference that the Son is begotten and the Father is unbegotten. This is where Athanasius applied the crucial term *homoousios*, that which was legitimized in the ecumenical Council of Nicaea 325 AD. A local synod was convened In Alexandria 362 AD in which Athanasius affirmed the distinction of the three *hypostases* of the Father, the Son, and the Holy Spirit.[56] This was an important step to refute any Sabellian claims—that of modalism—in adhering to the term *homoousios*.[57] The three *hypostases* are not manifestations of *one personal God but rather are distinct persons*.[58] While refuting Sabellianism, it also must not adopt Marcion's tritheism. Concerning this latter point,

---

[54] Ibid.
[55] Roger E. Olson, *The Story of Christian Theology: Twenty Centuries of Tradition Reform* (Downers Grove: IVP Academic, 1999), 172.
[56] Ibid., 166.
[57] Ibid.
[58] Ibid.

Athanasius quotes the words of Dionysius of Rome who warns against severing the Divine Monarchy into three separate subsistences and three godheads.[59] Athanasius speaks of the Father's monarchy towards Christ in the context of the economy, but to both of them is attributed the "one dignity of Godhead."[60] Kallistos Ware presumes that the Cappadocian fathers were more effective in accentuating the distinction between the essence and the person than Athanasius did.[61]

The Cappadocians

The Cappadocian fathers—Basil, Gregory of Nyssa, and Gregory of Nazianzus—were close friends of Athanasius and were greatly influenced by his theology. Taking the endeavor of blotting-out Sabellianism and Arianism, as further discussed below, the Cappadocians built on what Athanasius' foundation. They were not the first to think of the Trinity as Divine persons but rather it was Tertullian.[62] John Wilks argues that, contrary to what is universally believed, the Cappadocians identified the one

---

[59] *Select Treatises of S. Athanasius, Archbishop of Alexandria, In Controversy with the Arians, Translated with Notes and Indices,* John Henry Newman, trans. (Oxford: Rivingtons, 1877), 45.
[60] Athanasius, *Historia Arianorum, NPNF* 2/4: 266-306.
[61] *The Ecumenical Legacy of the Cappadocians,* Nicu Dumitraşcu, ed. (New York: Palgrave Macmillan, 2015), 2.
[62] Kevin N. Giles, *Jesus and the Father: Modern Evangelicals Reinvent the Doctrine of the Trinity* (Grand Rapids: Zondervan Academic, 2009), 149.

ousia as the center of unity of God.[63] Where some theologians, like John Zizioulas, may infer that the Cappadocians implied that the person of the Father is the principle of God's unity. Basil contributed this important formula: "what is common refers to the being, while the hypostasis or person is the personal sign of what is specific or particular."[64] The Cappadocian fathers stressed the priority of personhood and that it is what explains the essence and not vice versa.[65] Gregory of Nyssa believed that the essence of God is beyond comprehension and he understood *ousia* as the commonly shared attributes of the Trinity, but still, there is diversity in persons.[66] In his Thirty-Eighth letter to Gregory of Nyssa, Basil explains the difference between *ousia* and *hypostasis*. For Basil, the *ousia* is the essence while the *hypostasis* is the person, the "identity."[67] In Greek philosophy the two terms may be regarded as synonyms.[68] His interpretation of Hebrews 1:3 is quite remarkable, taking the Son to be "the express image" of the person of the Father and not of the Godhead, i.e. the essence.[69] The person of the Son is a particular identity that is distinct from the person of the Father, and at

---

[63] Ibid.
[64] *The Ecumenical Legacy of the Cappadocians*, Ibid., 22.
[65] Ted Peters, *God as Trinity: Relationality and Temporality in Divine Life* (Louisville: Westminster John Knox Press, 1993), 34.
[66] Olson, *The Story of Christian Theology*, 180.
[67] Basil, *The Sacred Writings of Saint Basil,* (Alternmünster: Jazzybee Verlag, 2012), 357.
[68] Olson, *The Story of Christian Theology*, 185.
[69] Basil, *The Sacred Writings of Saint Basil,* 365.

the same time, the Father is manifested through the Son. According to the theology of the Cappadocians, the being is never detached from the *hypostasis*, in other words, "there is no unhypostasiated being."[70] Gregory Nazianzen corroborated the concept of *relatio* in God; there is only one being and three inter-related hypostases.[71]

Augustine of Hippo

Born 354 CE in a town called Thagste, in modern day Algeria.[72] Augustine is thought to have finished his treatise *De Trinitate* between 420 and 425.[73] Thomas Marsh conveys Augustine's main objectives to pen this masterpiece: 1) to state and explain the church's basic doctrine of the Trinity 2) to demonstrate that the doctrine of the Trinity as taught by the church is firmly grounded in the Scripture 3) to work out the peculiar rules of human language and logic that must be observed if the church is to speak of the Triune God 4) to attempt to discover in the highest form of creation immediately known to us, the human mind or spirit, vestiges of the Triune God who is its Origin and Creator.[74] Marsh and Gunton point to Augustine's error in founding his Trinitarian theology on

---

[70] *The Ecumenical Legacy of the Cappadocians*, Ibid., 29.
[71] Olson, *The Story of Christian Theology*, 187.
[72] Peter Brown, *Augustine of Hippo: A Biography,* (Oakland: University of California Press, 2000), 7.
[73] Lewis Ayres, *Augustine and the Trinity* (Cambridge: Cambridge University Press, 2010), 119.
[74] Olson and Hall, *The Trinity*, 44.

the unity of the Divine essence.[75] Marsh views that Augustine, contrary to the Latin tradition of holding a monarchy of the Father, understood "one God" to mean the Divine essence.[76] According to Marsh, this understanding severs the notions of the essence and the person, presenting an impersonal concept of God.[77] Gunton, in his criticism of Augustine, accuses him of not being able to comprehend the Trinitarian theology of "his predecessors" both in the West and the East, being influenced by Neoplatonism.[78] The Cappadocians were more successful in preserving the inter-relatedness between the Father, Son, and Spirit being, based in the ontology of God, according to Gunton.[79] He further points out Augustine's misconception in holding a "relation as a logical rather than an ontological predicate[…]"[80] The outcome, then, becomes the dissolution of the "distinguishable identity" into the oneness of God.[81] On the other hand, other scholars do not agree with Marsh and Gunton concerning Augustine.[82] Cary, for example, views that Augustine built the achievements of the Cappadocians.[83]

---

[75] Ibid.
[76] Ibid.
[77] Ibid.
[78] Ibid.
[79] Ibid.
[80] Ibid., 45.
[81] Ibid.
[82] Ibid.
[83] Ibid.

Controversies within the Ancient Catholic Church

Sabellius

A native of Rome and a contemporary to Zephyrinus of Rome (198-217 AD). Sabellius' teachings were very popular in North Africa by the fourth century; he may be considered the father of monarchic modalism.[84] Harnack suggests that Sabellius was born in Pentapolis, Libya.[85] Olson views that Sabellius revived the innovation of Praxeas.[86] Sabellius is vividly a proponent of monotheism. Marcellus of Ancyra seems to be in line with the thought of Sabellius to a certain extent and tried to revive Sabellianism.[87] Modalism is one feature of monotheism.[88] Sabellianism taught that the Father, the Son, and the Holy Spirit are manifestations of the one God. Sabellius was concerned that Christianity would be stuck with the scandalous accusation of worshiping three gods.[89] Origen viewed that the problem with the doctrine of Sabellius was depriving the Father and the Son of having to different

---

[84] Eusebius Pamphilius, *Church History*, NPNF 2/1: 81-402.
[85] Adolf Harnack, *History of Dogma*, Vol. 1 (Eugene: Wipf and Stock Publishers, 1997), 83.
[86] Olson, *The Story of Christian Theology*, 92.
[87] Isaak August Dorner, *History of the Development of the Doctrine of the Person of Christ* (Edinburggh: T. & T. Clark, 1889), 271.
[88] Moltmann, *The Trinity and the Kingdom*, 135.
[89] Harnack, *History of Dogma*, 85.

hypostases, ultimately merging them.[90] Sabellianism, according to Basil, posed a threat to the *hypostatic* or personal existence of the Holy Trinity.[91] Sabellianism gives way to *patripassionism*, a term that was coined by Tertullian,[92] it was God the Father, in the form of Jesus Christ, who incarnated and was crucified.[93] Collectively, Sabellianism taught that the Father and Son's unity is based upon having the same essence, i.e. being consubstantial, but with no *hypostatic* differentiation. Moltmann stresses that though this sequence of ideas may present an apparent attempt for preserving Christ's Divinity, nevertheless, what is affected is the complete vanishing of Christ in the Godhead.[94] Thus, within this theological framework, there is no place for Trinitarian communion and love. God appears as a prisoner of his solitude and oneness before creation, where his attributes and activity remain frozen.

Paul of Samosata

He was the bishop of Antioch from 260 AD to 268 AD. Paul understood the Logos as an "attribute" of the One God.[95] This attribute is named "Wisdom, Spirit or Logos."[96] Thus, Jesus Christ is the materialization of this attribute of

---

[90] Ibid., 84.
[91] John Behr, *The Nicene Faith* (Yonkers: SVS Press, 2004), 304.
[92] Olson, *The Story of Christian Theology*, 95.
[93] Moltmann, *The Trinity and the Kingdom*, 135.
[94] Ibid., 136.
[95] Ibid., 132.
[96] Ibid.

the Divine monad. Vividly, the theology of Paul of Samosata exhibits the features of subordinationism, but with a twist. Intending to preserve the unity of the Divine essence, Paul rejected the idea of Jesus being God.[97] Christ is a mere man through whom the Spirit works. Ultimately, Paul's perspective of the doctrine of the Trinity follows dynamic monarchianism rather than modalistic monarchianism.[98] The Logos is deprived of any personal aspects or possessing a *hypostasis* of his own.[99] Paul was overthrown of his bishopric at a local council in Antioch in 269 AD, being charged with holding the wrong "identity" of the Son of God.[100]

Arius

He was a Libyan priest, who died in 336 AD. He appears to have been a pupil of Lucian of Antioch.[101] Arius, too, was occupied with the idea of preserving the unity of God. Thus, his flow of thought commences from the One God, featuring subordinationism.[102] Jesus Christ was created by God as a mediator between Him and Creation. Regrettably, "Arianism is monotheistic Christianity in its purest

---

[97] Justo L. González, *A History of Christian Thought: From the Beginnings to the Council of Chalcedon* (Abingdon Press, 1987), 228.
[98] Ibid.
[99] Ibid.
[100] John Behr, *The Way to Nicaea* (Yonkers: SVS Press, 2001), 208.
[101] Rowan Williams, *Arius: Heresy and Tradition* (Norwich: SCM Press, 2001), 30.
[102] Moltmann, *The Trinity and the Kingdom*, 133.

form."[103] In the famous Council of Nicaea of 325 AD, Arius was condemned and his views were judged as heretical. Moltmann, expressing the outcome of the council, resembled in legitimizing the term *homousios*, views that now "identifying Christ with God and God with Christ," puts an end to monadic monotheism.[104]

Modern Perspectives of the Holy Trinity

Karl Barth

Under the subtitle "Trinitarian Monarchy," Jürgen Moltmann, analyzes Barth's doctrine of the Holy Trinity.[105] God as a subject precedes the Trinity and is revealed through the Trinity.[106] The ultimate concern for Barth is, again, preserving the unity of God, as his paradigm starts from the one Godhead and then moves to the Trinity, reproducing "Christian Monotheism."[107] Thus, in God, abstract existence foreshadows the ontological one. God's essence is expressed in the Trinity, and the essence attains autonomy. Though Barth labored to scrub any stains of Sabellianism in his doctrine, this never proved successful. Barth's paradigm of revelation closely resembles Sabellius' paradigm of manifestation. Both paradigms are founded on

---

[103] Ibid.
[104] Ibid., 134.
[105] Ibid., 139.
[106] Ibid., 140.
[107] Ibid.

the notion of the unity of the common essence. LaCugna emphasizes that Barth's doctrine is another model of modalism.[108] Moltmann specifies it as Sabellian modalism.[109] To this opinion, E.P. Meijering also agrees.[110] On the other hand, Rowan Williams and Eberhard Jungel hold that Barth's doctrine is free from Sabellianism.[111] What is evident is that Barth deprived the Trinity of any true personal existence, but rather, the Trinity are "modes of being."[112] This line of thought that extends to the theology of Karl Rahner.

Karl Rahner

The renowned theologian of the twentieth century agrees with Barth that, in God, there is only one Divine subject. Rahner repudiates any personal reciprocity in God.[113] There is only one "I" which belongs to the one nature. Unfortunately, Rahner's theology is founded on his impaired anthropology. Holding a reduced understating of the *person*, Rahner, confuses it with *individual*.[114]

---

[108] John Webster, *The Cambridge Companion to Karl Barth* (Cambridge: Cambridge University Press, 2000), 83.
[109] Ibid., 84.
[110] Prof Dr Rinse H. Reeling Brouwer, *Karl Barth and Post-Reformation Orthodoxy* (Burlington: Ashgate Publishing, Ltd., 2015), 227.
[111] Webster, *The Cambridge Companion to Karl Barth*, 84.
[112] Moltmann, *The Trinity and the Kingdom*, 143.
[113] Thomas McCall, *Which Trinity? Whose Monotheism? Philosophical and Systematic Theologians on the Metaphysics of Trinitarian Theology* (Wm. B. Eerdmans Publishing, 2010), 89.
[114] Moltmann, *The Trinity and the Kingdom*, 145.

Contrastively, Zizioulas makes great emphasis on the relational aspect of the person. An individual, properly understood, resembles an independent identity or existence, a subsistence. Individuality, in turn, resembles a horrific element that breaks the unity of God. Again, it seems that Rahner in his endeavor to preserve God's unity slips into modalism. The Divine subject is attributed to the essence, the Trinity are merely modes of beings of the one subject or rather three "modes of subsistence."[115]

John Zizioulas

Zizioulas' doctrine of God proved to give excessive attention to the notion of the person, and consequently the notion of *relational ontology*. It is thought of as being mainly Trinitarian theology. In fact, Zizioulas' approach to the doctrine of God is quite impressive, being "enthusiastically adopted by all theologians."[116] Nevertheless, Zizioulas is criticized concerning his inclination toward Monarchianism. Kärkkäinen presents the echoing question of whether Zizioulas was able to capture the Cappadocians' theology of the Trinity accurately, precisely on "asymmetrical reciprocity among the Trinitarian members."[117] Truly the Church fathers spoke of the Father as the cause of the Son and the Holy Spirit. But

---

[115] Leonardo Boff, *Trinity and Society* (Maryknoll: Orbis Books, 1988), 137.
[116] Veli-Matti Kärkkäinen, *The Trinity: Global Perspectives* (Louisville: Presbyterian Publishing Corp, 2007), 96.
[117] Ibid., 97.

Zizioulas deeply implies the monarchy of the Father. Volf inquires on the connection between conserving the unity of God and the monarchy of the Father in Zizioulas' paradigm.[118] Put in Leonardo Boff's words: "even if its starting point is personalized [the Person of the Father], this theology is in fact one of essence and of divine unity, centered on the first Person."[119] Alan Torrance goes to the point of charging Zizioulas with subordinationism, where the Father attains the primordial ontological reality.[120] Further, he points to Zizioulas' integration of ecclesiology and anthropology in connection to his Trinitarian theology.[121] Torrance decries Zizioulas' failure to appreciate the notion of Divine unity in communion and resorting to a causal principle (the Father).[122] Also, Zizioulas holds that "the being of God is identified with the person."[123] Zizioulas himself is aware of how this *monarchia* has "acquired a pejorative sense" in modern scholarship.[124] Alan criticizes Zizioulas' idea of self-transcendence that God's unity is effectuated through the

---

[118] Miroslav Volf, *After Our Likeness: The Church as the Image of the Trinity* (Grand Rapids: Wm. B. Eerdmans Publishing, 1998), 79.
[119] Boff, *Trinity and Society*, 137.
[120] Alan Torrance, *Persons in Communion: Trinitarian Description and Human Participation* (London: A&C Black, 1996), 92, 93.
[121] Ibid., 295.
[122] Ibid., 289.
[123] Alan Torrance, *Persons in Communion: Trinitarian Description and Human Participation* (London: A&C Black, 1996), 289.
[124] John D. Zizioulas, *Communion and Otherness: Further Studies in Personhood and the Church* (New York: Bloomsbury Publishing, 2010), 143.

"perichoretic communion of persons participating in the triune, personal life of God."[125] Again, this last phrase implies a personal onticity of the Godhead, as if the consummation of the Trinity results in a monadic personified essence. If a being in *ekstasis* departs his hypostasis,[126] as Zizioulas presumes, what then is left of him? Does this idea signify hypostatic dissolution? Is not *perichoresis* a process that demands personal participation? Ultimately, Zizioulas' doctrine of God is primarily Trinitarian, outwardly and linguistically, but substantially exhibits monarchianism, for the sake of Divine unity that is founded on the essence of the Father.[127] Shockingly, Zizioulas is philosophizing the notion of person through anthropology,[128] demoting the divine persons.

The Torrances[129]

Alan Torrance is a proponent of his uncle's (T. F. Torrance) Trinitarian theology.[130] Torrance agrees with Zizioulas on conceiving *Being* in personal terms, where this

---

[125] Torrance, *Persons in Communion*, 301.
[126] John D. Zizioulas, "Human Capacity and Human Incapacity: A Theological Exploration of Personhood1," *Scottish Journal of Theology* 28, no. 5 (October 1975): 408, doi:10.1017/S003693060003533X.
[127] John D. Zizioulas, *Being as Communion: Studies in Personhood and the Church* (Yonkers: SVS Press, 1985), 41.
[128] Zizioulas, "Human Capacity and Human Incapacity," 408.
[129] The 'Torrances' signifies Thomas F. Torrance and Alan J. Torrance.
[130] Ralph Del Colle, "'Person' and 'Being' in John Zizioulas' Trinitarian Theology: Conversations with Thomas Torrance and Thomas Aquinas," *Scottish Journal of Theology* 54, no. 1 (February 2001): 72.

is the resolution to avoid confusing *methexis* (Platonic participation) with *koinonia*.[131] But the difference is that he holds the monarchy equally shared by the three Divine persons,[132] and in this, he is also in agreement with Thomas F. Torrance.[133] Alan even quotes his uncle's usage of Cyril of Alexandria's *"mia arche."*[134] Zizioulas criticizes Alan Torrance on separating *personhood* from *being* and linking the latter to *ousia*.[135] Zizioulas reasons that this is the exact point that makes the monarchy of the Father problematic for Torrance.[136] This illustrates how Torrance dresses the essence of God with an ontological *emballage*. According to George Dragas, Torrance is subordinating *hypostasis* to *ousia*, and that the latter assumed that Athanasius never spoke of the Father as being the cause of the Son.[137] Dragas is objecting to T.F. Torrance's claim that the Godhead (*ousia*) is a person, the matter that appears in the "Agreed Statement on the Holy Trinity."[138] Consequently, the Trinity's personhood is demoted, as they are robbed from constituting God's being hypostatically. Zizioulas is in disagreement with Torrance on that the ultimate reality of

---

[131] Torrance, *Persons in Communion*, 362.
[132] Colle, Ibid., 79.
[133] Torrance, *Persons in Communion*, 291.
[134] Ibid., 294.
[135] Zizioulas, *Communion and Otherness*, 125.
[136] Ibid.
[137] Matthew Baker and Todd H. Speidell, *T. F. Torrance and Eastern Orthodoxy: Theology in Reconciliation* (Eugene: Wipf and Stock Publishers, 2015), 17.
[138] Ibid.

God is to be found in His intra-Divine communion.[139] This idea speaks of abstract concepts in an ontological manner. Gunton criticizes Thomas Torrance's inclination toward the diminution of the "particularity of the hypostasis" and overemphasizing the "homogeneity of the being."[140] In this Torrance is following the Western trend in order to preserve God's unity, notes Gunton.[141] According to Dragas, T.F. Torrance views that the Son is born of the Father's essence and is one with the Father in essence.[142] Torrance is depending here on the Creed of Nicaea that states, "*ek tes ousias tou Patros,*" this phrase was later modified in the Creed of Constantinople to "*ek tou Patros.*"[143] Contrastively, Zizioulas stresses that this change manifests the truth that the person of the Father is the cause of the Trinity as opposed to the essence.[144] Thus, Torrance, in the act of refuting Zizioulas, subordinated the hypostasis to the one essence.[145]

---

[139] Zizioulas, *Communion and Otherness*, 134.
[140] C. Gunton, review of *Trinitarian Perspectives. Towards Doctrinal Agreement*, by Thomas F. Torrance. *Scottish Journal of Theology* 52, no. 3 (August 1999): 379-380, https://doi.org/10.1017/S0036930600050298.
[141] Ibid., 379.
[142] Baker and Speidell, *T. F. Torrance and Eastern Orthodoxy*, 16.
[143] Colle, "'Person' and 'Being' in John Zizioulas' Trinitarian Theology," 70.
[144] Ibid., 71.
[145] Baker and Speidell, *T. F. Torrance and Eastern Orthodoxy*, 17.

Conclusion

This sweeping survey across the history of the doctrine of God can be summarized as follows:

- The Doctrine of the Holy Trinity was developed within the context of theological controversies.
- The fathers of the fourth century were mainly concerned with purifying the doctrine of God from abstract philosophical paradigms, preserving it as a mystery.[146]
- The unity of God is the most problematic and daunting notion to the Christian consciousness, this is of course in addition to the concept of monarchy.[147]
- There are two main worldviews of the doctrine of God. First, the one that starts from the unity and ends with Trinity, from abstract existence to the ontological. Second, the one that begins from the Trinity and ends with unity, ontological existence negates what is abstract.
- Theological models that are founded on and begin from the unity of the one essence are prone to give way to monarchianism or modalism.
- Not every theological model that is using Trinitarian terminology is being purely Trinitarian, but they may prove to be otherwise.

---

[146] Olson, *The Story of Christian Theology*, 174.
[147] Moltmann, *The Trinity and the Kingdom*, 139.

- The traditional background of the theologian must be kept in mind when interpreting his doctrine, thus finding a common plane of thought with him.
- Most of the innovations, that occurred through the course of the history of the Church, were a direct outcome of implementing abstract philosophical concepts apart from Church tradition. This proves to be true even if the innovator's original intent was virtuous.
- Previous innovations may be reproduced later in time using new terminologies and different theological paradigms.
- With time, some of the theological terminologies acquired new meanings, others were newly coined, and some were fixated in meaning.
- Terminology is applied with variations in meaning within the theological dialogues. Though one term can be universally understood in philosophy, it might have a special usage in some traditions.

Cyril's Ontological Priority of Personhood

Cyril of Alexandria: An Archetype of the Alexandrian Theology

The catechetical school of Alexandria was instituted in the year 195 AD by Clement of Alexandria.[148] This ancient and famous theological school maintained a *Logos-Sarx* Christological worldview,[149] in contrast to the Antiochene *Logos-Anthropos* Christology. Nevertheless, Cyril affirms, in his exegetical work on the Gospel of John, that "and the Word became flesh" (Joh 1:14) typically means that the Word became man (*Anthropos*). The main idea behind this paradigm is the preservation of the identity of the Son of God, who in the fulness of time incarnated.[150] Incarnated, Jesus Christ remains the same person of the Word of God. The Word did not unite himself to a chosen man, who existed before the first moment of the incarnation. Cyril of Alexandria, of course, was a custodian of the Alexandrian tradition and also observed the works of the earlier fathers with respect. Cyril incorporated the works of Clement of

---

[148] Thomas P. Rausch, *Who Is Jesus? An Introduction to Christology* (Liturgical Press, 2003), 153.
[149] Weinandy and Keating, *The Theology of St. Cyril of Alexandria*, 28.
[150] Rausch, *Who Is Jesus?*, 153.

Alexandria, Didymus, and other Alexandrian fathers in his writings.[151]

Concerning philosophy, Cyril of Alexandria was often critical of Aristotelian philosophy and Stoicism, but this did not prevent him from using its dialect at times in a causal way.[152] De Ghellinck states that Cyril "had been so severe on Aristotle."[153] He believed that his terminology must be understandable to his opponents. In his *Thesaurus*, Cyril shows acuity in treating Aristotelian logic.[154]

Ultimately, Cyril the Great had sharp awareness of the different philosophical terms of his time and was able to employ them in the right context, making them understandable and familiar as possible to his opponents. For him "logic is a tool to be used with flexibility and creativity" says Siddals.[155] Cyril was able to use Aristotelian logic in both his Trinitarian and Christological writings, according to Siddals and Boulnois,[156] and this was mainly against the heretics.[157] This was a consequence owed to the fact that the heretics "attack us on the basis of Aristotle's teachings" according to Cyril.[158]

---

[151] Loon, *The Dyophysite Christology of Cyril of Alexandria*, 63.
[152] Ibid.
[153] van Loon, *The Dyophysite Christology of Cyril of Alexandria*, 68.
[154] Ibid., 64.
[155] Ibid.
[156] Ibid., 69.
[157] Ibid., 68.
[158] van Loon, *The Dyophysite Christology of Cyril of Alexandria*, 94.

The Christology of Cyril of Alexandria

The writings of Cyril were mainly propelled by a fixed concern with soteriology.[159] This was concomitantly fulfilled by his exegetical works and the person of Jesus Christ, as the Savior and the mediator of the Divine economy, became Cyril's driving force in writing. Everything, in the heavens and on earth, revolves around the incarnate Son of God. For the patriarch, Christ is a mystery; he describes the Incarnation of our Lord as a great mystery.[160] The following words, from the *Interpretation of John*, exhibit Cyril's Christological core: "while giving life as God by his all-powerful command, He also gives life by the touch of his holy flesh, demonstrating through both that the operation was a *single* and cognate one."[161] In Jesus there is only one person, the Son of God, who incarnated uniting himself to a full humanity. This is what can be called Cyril's "singular activity" of Christ. Consequently, it was not acceptable for Cyril to perceive Nestorius' dualistic Christology. Nestorius argued for a dichotomy between Christ's Divinity and humanity. Posing questions in the likeness of "does God suffer?" Weinandy discusses Cyril's "communication of idioms" and concludes that for Cyril, Christ is a single "ontological entity," that is of the Son of God.[162] Cyril's *communicatio idiomatum* is based on the

---

[159] Weinandy and Keating, *The Theology of St. Cyril of Alexandria*, 24.
[160] Loon, *The Dyophysite Christology of Cyril of Alexandria*, 398.
[161] Weinandy and Keating, *The Theology of St. Cyril of Alexandria*, 30.
[162] Ibid.

hypostatic union that took place at the event of the Incarnation. In this, O'Keefe views that the Alexandrians were more faithful to the scriptural tradition than the Antiochenes, who in turn were inclined to interpret the Scriptures according to philosophy.[163] Cyril's explanation of *Anathema Two* reveals his understanding of John 1:14 and how he remains faithful to the biblical *Logos/Sarx* model:

> "It means that the Word of God the Father became flesh, not by a change or alteration of his own nature, as we have already said, but because having made the flesh taken from the holy Virgin his own, one and the same subject is called Son, before the Incarnation as Word still incorporeal and after the Incarnation as the same Word now embodied. That is why we say that the same subject is simultaneously both God and man, not dividing him conceptually into a human being with a separate individual identity and God the Word also with a separate identity, that we may exclude any idea of two Sons, but acknowledging that one and the same subject is Christ and Son and Lord."[164]

---

[163] Ibid., 31.
[164] Norman Russell, *Cyril of Alexandria*, (New York: Routledge, 2000), 179.

But more importantly, the latter paragraph speaks of the incarnational becoming, illustrating Cyril's ontological Christology and how the person is given center stage. The person is the *subject* who bears a persistent *identity*, that removes unmoved throughout and after the process of incarnation. Cyril's Christology dominantly takes a realistic and ontological stance rather than being philosophical or conceptual. Weinandy describes Cyril's comprehension of the Incarnation as "a personal/existential conception."[165]

According to Cyril's view, there are two essences and one hypostasis. Nevertheless, the patriarch's full Christology is revealed through his application of the term *physis*.

Nature (physis) in the Theology of Cyril

The term nature (*physis*) appears to have a multifaceted meaning in the theology and language of Cyril. The following is an illustration for this matter:

> "It was not otherwise possible for man, forasmuch as he was of a nature that was perishing, to escape death, save by recovering that ancient grace, and partaking once more in God Who holdeth all things together in being and preserveth them in life through the Son in the Spirit. Therefore, He hath become partaker of blood and flesh, i.e. He hath become man, being

---

[165] Weinandy and Keating, *The Theology of St. Cyril of Alexandria*, 43.

by nature Life, and begotten of the Life that is by nature, i.e. of God the Father—to wit, His Only-begotten Word, with intent that ineffably and inexpressibly and as He alone could skill to do, uniting Himself with the flesh that by the law of its own nature was perishing, He might bring it back unto His own Life and make it through Himself partaker of God the Father."[166]

In this paragraph, Cyril speaks of two natures. The perishing nature of man, and the nature of the only-begotten Word, which in turn is of the Father's nature. It should be pointed here that the term nature in man's "nature that was perishing," contrasted to the Word who is by "nature life," mainly speaks of a "mode of life." In other words, *nature* is understood as "mode of life" and not as *essence*. This meaning is more emphasized by the phrase "by the law of its own nature was perishing." If nature is taken to mean *essence*, this will make the human essence to be perishing.

Through the notion of the "incarnational becoming," it appears that Cyril is primarily focusing on the ontology of the Word.[167] The only begotten Son united himself ontologically to the human essence: "the Word is God by nature both in the flesh and with the flesh since he has it as his own property."[168] According to Weinandy,

---

[166] Cyril of Alexandria, *Commentary on John*, trans. Members of the English Church, vol. 2 (London: W. Smith, 1885), chap. 14:20.
[167] Weinandy and Keating, *The Theology of St. Cyril of Alexandria*, 28.
[168] Russell, *Cyril of Alexandria*, 106.

Cyril used the analogy of the human soul/body union to explain how an ontological union results in one reality or entity.[169] The Logos incarnated in human flesh to form one ontological reality, that of Jesus Christ. The Subject of the Son is the center of attention. Cyril, in his *Commentary on Isaiah*, illustrates how attributes, both Divine and human, are assigned to the Son by the prophet Isaiah,[170] emphasizes the ontological priority of the person of the Word.[171] Accordingly, Cyril states in his *Contra Nestorius*:

> "For the nature (φύσις) of the Incarnate Word himself is immediately, after the union, conceived as one (μία). It is not unreasonable to see something similar in our own case too. For a human being is truly one compounded of dissimilar elements, by which I mean soul and body."[172]
>
> "Accordingly, all the sayings contained in the Gospels must be referred to a single person (ἑνί προσώπῳ), to the one incarnate subject (ὑποστάσει) of the Word;"

---

[169] Weinandy and Keating, *The Theology of St. Cyril of Alexandria*, 33.
[170] Russell, *Cyril of Alexandria*, 79.
[171] Weinandy and Keating, *The Theology of St. Cyril of Alexandria*, 28.
[172] Weinandy and Keating, *The Theology of St. Cyril of Alexandria*, 35.

In this statement Cyril uses *prosopon* and *hypostasis* in replacement of *physis*.[173]

Emmanuel Gergis emphasizes that Cyril, as his predecessor Athanasius, takes *physis* to mean *one reality* within the context of Christology.[174] Hence Cyril is in line with the Alexandrian tradition concerning this usage of *physis*. Gergis then quotes Van Loon indicating that *physis*, *hypostasis*, and *prospopon* are synonymous in the Christological writings of Cyril, designating a subsistence.[175] Though Cyril might use the *physis* in the sense of quiddity when addressing human nature in general, still, he preserves *physis* as reality to the Christological dialogue.[176]

Another important expression that Cyril uses to describe the *hypostatic* union in Christ is *kata physin*, or "according to nature." This idiom indicates that the union that took place in the incarnation was achieved in the ontological plane of the person of the Logos. Consequently "according to nature," *kata physin*, in Cyril is equivalent to "according to person" (καθ᾽ ὑπόστασιν).[177]

---

[173] Ibid., 38.
[174] Gergis, Ibid., 274.
[175] Ibid.
[176] Weinandy and Keating, *The Theology of St. Cyril of Alexandria*, 38.
[177] Ibid., 41.

Cyril's Christological Formula

For Cyril, a definition is a formula, a λόγος.[178] A definition must only include affirmations and be void of any negations.[179] Cyril's popular and ever-dominating Christological formula i.e., defining who Christ is, states: "μία φύσις τοῦ θεοῦ λόγου σεσαρκωμένη" or "one enfleshed nature of the Word,"[180] Christ is one nature, because two natures, for Cyril, meant two distinguished realities or subsistences.[181] For *physis* in Cyril's Christological formula is synonymous to *prosopon*, a person.[182] Joseph van den Dries argues that *physis* in the μία φύσις formula corresponds to *physis-prosopon* as it pertains to the person of the Logos.[183] Gergis stresses: "Cyril understood μία φύσις to mean the reality of the union of the divine with the human in the one person of Christ."[184] Eventually, the Christological formula is answering the question of who is Christ. This question demands a subject to be determined and then it continues to define who the one reality is, the mode according to which this one subject be existent.[185]

---

[178] Loon, *The Dyophysite Christology of Cyril of Alexandria*, 100.
[179] Ibid., 103.
[180] John McGuckin, *St. Cyril of Alexandria: The Christological Controversy: Its History, Theology, and Texts* (Leiden: Brill, 1994), 208.
[181] Loon, *The Dyophysite Christology of Cyril of Alexandria*, 16.
[182] Ibid.
[183] Ibid., 17.
[184] Baker and Speidell, *T. F. Torrance and Eastern Orthodoxy*, 274.
[185] Weinandy and Keating, *The Theology of St. Cyril of Alexandria*, 38.

Though Cyril's Christological formula speaks of one nature; at the same time, it is aware of the union between the Divine and human essences. Thus, the worldview behind this formula is that of maintaining the ontological priority of personhood. In the person lies the true reality of the being. The person is the ultimate reality. There is no speaking of an essence that precedes the person. The essence, then, is secondary to the person. A person exhibits a certain essence. Essences do not outgrow persons. The Son of God (the person) incarnated, i.e. acquired a human essence. Cyril stresses that the humanity of Jesus was not that of an ordinary man where the Logos "simply settled on him."[186] Consequently, the incarnation was not the union of abstract essences, but rather the outcome of the activity of the second person of the Holy Trinity.

So though one attributes the nature of manhood and of Godhead to Emmanuel, the manhood has become the Word's own and together with it is seen as one Son.[187] The center of focus here, again, is the *hypostasis* of the Word of God, who in Him the *hypostatic* union takes place. Weinandy explicates that Cyril's sole intention in the latter quotation is that Christ is one entity, for him "Christ is one."[188] Therefore the *mia physis* stands in affirmation of his one reality, in contrast to one quiddity.[189] And this one entity is the person/subject (*prosopon/hypostasis*) of the

---

[186] Weinandy and Keating, *The Theology of St. Cyril of Alexandria*, 32.
[187] Weinandy and Keating, *The Theology of St. Cyril of Alexandria*, 35.
[188] Ibid.
[189] Ibid.

Son of God existing as man.[190] Vividly, for Cyril, *prosopon* and *hypostasis* are synonyms to *physis* within Christology. The one ontological person of Christ in Cyril's writings is employed to refute the dualistic Christology of his opponents.[191] Cyril's opponents are mainly interested in secondary substances that make up Christ but Cyril's theology is purely ontological, in contrast to the other's mechanical and abstract philosophical thinking. Consequently, Cyril's main conflict with Nestorius was the latter's language that implied the union between two persons in Christ.

> "As for our Savior's statements in the Gospels, we do not divide them out to two subjects (ὑπόστασις) or persons (πρόσωποις). The one, unique Christ has no duality though he is seen as compounded in inseparable unity out of two (ἐκ δύο) differing elements in the way that a human being, for example, is seen to have no duality but to be one (εἰς) consisting of the pair of elements, body and soul."[192]

In the above passage, it appears that Cyril's main concern is to be found in the notion of the person, the ontological entity. The patriarch's response is directed towards refuting Nestorius. This was a response to

---

[190] Ibid., 39.
[191] Loon, *The Dyophysite Christology of Cyril of Alexandria*, 510.
[192] Weinandy and Keating, *The Theology of St. Cyril of Alexandria*, 34.

Nestorius' usage of the "two natures." On the other hand, for the Antiochenes "one nature" meant a single "quiddity" where the two essences, that of the man and the Divine, are compounded together.[193] This is revealed in Nestorius' reply to Cyril, where he says that Cyril turned the Divine *ousia* of Christ into the *ousia* of man, and the *ousia* of man to that of God.[194] Ultimately, the Antiochene recognition of what a being is finds its answer in the notion of the essence. The Antiochene worldview is lacking the ontological perspective, rather it is more focused on the abstract existence of the substances. Accordingly, the Antiochene Christology gives priority to the notion of the essence. Cyril cannot accept two natures, where nature denotes, in Cyril's view, *what he is*, and this in turn is an ontological question for Cyril. Enforcing this latter understanding, Cyril insisted that the attributes are to be predicated of the person and not of the essences, where the "incarnational becoming" is "*kath' hypostasin.*"[195]

Cyril's ontological priority of personhood is profoundly manifested in his defense of the Virgin Mary's title the *Theotokos*. Mary is the mother of the Son of God. Clearly, the patriarch's definition of *who Mary is* is the outcome to his ontologically founded perspective of *who Christ is*. Consequently, the person of the Word of God has suffered and died in the flesh "for our sake" according to

---

[193] Ibid., 33.
[194] Ibid.
[195] Ibid., 47.

Cyril's Twelfth Anathema.[196] Therefore Christ's reality is Him being the second person of the Holy Trinity. Russell emphasizes that the controversy that took place between Cyril and Nestorius was not merely caused by conflicting terminology.[197] Rather it was a problem of varying Christological models, where Cyril maintained a single subject of Christ.[198] Concerning the Holy Trinity Cyril wrote extensively on that matter in his quest to refute the Arians and the Eunomians. Cyril maintained an ontological priority of personhood in the field of Trinitarian theology.

The Trinitarian Theology of Cyril

Cyril's writings on the Trinity preceded his Christological writings, but it is imperative for this study to first comprehend the dominance of the ontological priority of personhood in Cyril's worldview, through his Christological writings. The Pillar of Orthodoxy teaches that God is unknowable in His substance.[199] He usually refers to this aspect of God as the *ousia*. Nevertheless, Cyril's teaching was void of "the generic concept of the divine *ousia*."[200] The name "Father" denotes His begetting of the Son, while the name of the Son denotes Him being born of the Father.[201] Though Cyril refuses any causal

---

[196] Ibid., 48.
[197] Russell, *Cyril of Alexandria*, 41.
[198] Ibid.
[199] *Thesaurus de Trinitate,* 28A.
[200] Torrance, *Trinitarian Faith*, 338.
[201] Loon, *The Dyophysite Christology of Cyril of Alexandria*, 97.

relations—that one hypostasis is the cause and source of the other— within the Trinity,²⁰² still he might refer to the Father as the cause (ἀρχή) of the Son. The begetting of the Son is "the fruit of the hypostasis of the begetter."²⁰³ But by no means does this latter phrase hold any trace of subordination for Cyril, because Cyril refuted any subordinationism within the Holy Trinity. The Father is greater than the Son only according to economy. Cyril built on the Athanasian and Cappadocian teachings to produce a theology that plainly featured the "doctrine of the mutual indwelling of the three divine Persons in a rich doctrine of coinherence which deepened theological understanding of the Triunity of God."²⁰⁴ The names "Father" and "Son" designate a distinct prosopon for each.²⁰⁵ The knowledge of something is based on "what it is by nature" (κατα φύσιν), according to its reality (αληθώς).²⁰⁶ In his *Dialogues on the Trinity*, Cyril explains that the relationship within the Trinity is a *natural* relationship, i.e. according to nature, that is to say *inter-personal*.²⁰⁷ Cyril upholds the Creed of Faith, that the Son is of the same substance (ὁμοούσιος) of the Father.²⁰⁸ Once more, concerning this last point, Cyril is in line with his predecessor, Athanasius.²⁰⁹ The Son must be

---

²⁰² Torrance, *Trinitarian Faith*, 338.
²⁰³ Loon, *The Dyophysite Christology of Cyril of Alexandria*, 129.
²⁰⁴ Torrance, *Trinitarian Faith*, 338.
²⁰⁵ Loon, *The Dyophysite Christology of Cyril of Alexandria*, 97.
²⁰⁶ Ibid.
²⁰⁷ Russell, *Cyril of Alexandria*, 25.
²⁰⁸ Loon, *The Dyophysite Christology of Cyril of Alexandria*, 98.
²⁰⁹ Weinandy and Keating, *The Theology of St. Cyril of Alexandria*, 25.

God for the salvation of man to take place, noting that between the Father and the Son an ineffable union is to be found,[210] a union that concomitantly "conjoins and divides."[211] Thus, oneness in God does not denote singularity but rather a union in diversity. Although the Father and the Son are consubstantial, each has his separate *hypostasis*. Cyril indicates that the Son is equal to the Father "according to the formula of the substance."[212] While creatures acquire their relation to the Trinity through participation, the Son relates to the Father naturally (φυσικώς).[213] The coexistence of the Father and the Son is stressed as one of them cannot exist without the other.[214] Cyril uses the word σχεσεις to describe the ontological relation between the Father and the Son. The monarchy, for Cyril, consequently, is a "unity in Trinity" and a "Trinity in unity," where he disagreed with the Cappadocian causal relation within the Trinity.[215] Cyril adopted a Trinitarian understanding depending on

> "Three perfect, coequal, coeternal, enhypostatic Persons through their wholly reciprocal indwelling and containing of one another, in

---

[210] Loon, *The Dyophysite Christology of Cyril of Alexandria*, 99.
[211] Ibid., 126.
[212] van Loon, *The Dyophysite Christology of Cyril of Alexandria*, 99.
[213] Ibid., 113.
[214] Ibid., 120.
[215] Torrance, *Trinitarian Faith*, 339.

which they are inconfusedly united and inseparably distinguished."[216]

The latter concept was peculiar in holding at once the notions of *mia archia* and *mia ousia*.[217] According to Cyril, the Son and the Holy Spirit are both "in" and "from" the Father, they are simultaneously outside and inside the Father, the concept that paves the way for the upcoming notion of perichoresis.[218] Ultimately, Cyril's ontological priority of personhood is manifested in identifying the *Monarchia* with the Triunity of God:[219]

> "No one, I deem, rightly minded would suppose that the inbreathing which proceeded from the divine essence became the creature's soul, but that after the creature was ensouled, or rather had attained to the distinctive property of its perfect nature by means of both—I mean of course, soul and body—then like a seal of his own nature the Creator impressed on it the Holy Spirit, that is, the breath of life, through which it was being moulded to the archetypal beauty, and was being perfected according to the image of the one who created it, being established for every kind of excellence, by virtue of the Spirit given to dwell in it."[220]

---

[216] Ibid., 340.
[217] Ibid.
[218] Weinandy and Keating, *The Theology of St. Cyril of Alexandria*, 98.
[219] Torrance, *Trinitarian Faith*, 340.
[220] Weinandy and Keating, *The Theology of St. Cyril of Alexandria,* 154.

In the previous paragraph, Cyril of Alexandria in his *Commentary on the Gospel of John,* refutes the communication of the Divine essence from God to man. Rather he emphasizes the personal activity of the Holy Spirit. It is an action of the third hypostasis. Boulnois stress that for Cyril, God's being and action are inseparable and are manifested through the salvific activity of Christ and the Holy Spirit in history, where they reveal their proper mode of being.[221] This is another example of the patriarch's understanding of the Trinity's ontological priority of the person, as opposed to essence.

Conclusion

The Alexandrian tradition is vividly peculiar in its ontological perspective. The Church of Alexandria holds an ontological priority of personhood, where the person is the ultimate reality of the being. Thus, the purpose of discussing Cyril's Christological theology is mainly excavating his ontological priority of personhood. This ontological priority of personhood is further and by extension, applied to his Trinitarian theology. The core of Cyril's Trinitarian theology can be simplified according to his words:

> "The unique nature of the divinity is in three distinct hypostases, yet of a single form and of

---

[221] Ibid., 148.

identical essence, coming together into a unique, transcendent beauty."²²²

The question of what a being is by nature (κατα φύσιν), or its definition according to Cyril, finds its answer in the *person*. Cyril's Christological formula reveals his worldview, based on his understanding of the term *physis*, that the *hypostasis* or the *prosopon* manifests the reality of the being, i.e. what the being is. The person is the focal point of onticity, reality, and identity. This is contrasted to the Antiochene perspective that embraces the Aristotelian notion of the essence (secondary substance), and results in diophysite Christology as an outcome. When the ontological priority is given to the essence, the person is consequently subordinated to the essence. The person then loses its ontological significance and merely represents a certain quality in God. This can be found in the theology of Paul of Samosata and later in the ninth century by the Arab writer *Abū Rāi'ṭa Al-Takriti* in his treatise *On the Holy Trinity*. In this latter example, the hypostasis is described as a personal attribute in the one God. Unfortunately, this paradigm demotes Trinitarian theology for the sake of preserving the Divine unity and supplementing the monarchy. Subsequently, Persons do not comprise any ontological connotation but are reduced into qualities or attributes of the one essence. The latter is, contrastingly, spoken of in an ontological manner.

---

²²² Weinandy and Keating, *The Theology of St. Cyril of Alexandria*, 116.

Personhood Against Monarchianism in Modern Theological Dialogue

The Trinitarian Theology of the Torrances

In Contrast to the Ancient Catholic Church and Her Terminology

Thomas F. Torrance provides a very important treatise titled *The Trinitarian Faith*, and in this important work, he illustrates the patristic doctrine of the Holy Trinity. Torrance's own doctrine of the Holy Trinity seems consistent with the fourth and fifth centuries patristic views, especially that of the Cappadocians, Athanasius, and Epiphanius of Salamis.[223] Evidently, Thomas Torrance has a special affinity towards Athanasius' Trinitarian theology, whose worldview he adopts and through which he perceives the whole tradition.[224] This may explain Torrance's dependence on the term *homoousion*, especially in addressing the theme of the *monarchia*, the matter investigated by Asproulis.[225] He argues that Torrance is mainly articulating his thought depending on the notions of *homoousion* and

---

[223] Baker and Speidell, *T. F. Torrance and Eastern Orthodoxy*, 164.
[224] Ibid.
[225] Ibid., 163.

perichoresis.²²⁶ For Torrance, the *ousia* signifies the *Being* of God that communicates the reality of the *identity* of the Being between the persons of the Trinity.²²⁷ Thus the *ousia* has a revelatory function. According to Shepherd, Torrance's reliance on *homoousion* "safeguards [...] the Trinity against any form of Sabellianism or modalism, and the doctrine of God against any form of Unitarianism or polytheism."²²⁸ Asproulis sees that behind Torrance's occupation with *homoousion* is his conception that Arianism is the "most serious and primitive heresy."²²⁹ *Homoousion* for Torrance connotes at the same time the *one* and the *triune* God.²³⁰ Torrance views that Athanasius, through *homoousion*, established a doctrine of *monarchia* founded on "the one indivisible being of the Holy Trinity."²³¹ He goes further to hint at Basil's effort in "distinguishing properties of the three divine Persons."²³² But most importantly is that *homoousion* precludes any suggestion of subordinationism in the Holy Trinity; this at

---

²²⁶ Ibid.
²²⁷ Ibid.
²²⁸ "Thomas F. Torrance and the Homoousion of the Holy Spirit," *Participatio: Journal of the Thomas F. Torrance Theological Fellowship* 3 (2012): 108.
²²⁹ "T. F. Torrance and John Zizioulas on the Divine Monarchia: The Cappadocian Background and the Neo-Cappadocian Solution," *Participatio: Journal of the Thomas F. Torrance Theological Fellowship* 4 (2013): 165.
²³⁰ Colin E. Gunton, *Father, Son and Holy Spirit: Toward a Fully Trinitarian Theology*, 1 edition (London; New York: T & T Clark International, 2003), 34.
²³¹ Torrance, *Trinitarian Faith*, 10.
²³² Ibid.

the same time diminishes the monarchy of the Father.[233] On the other hand, Gunton strongly argues that it is Augustine who is most influential on Torrance's Trinitarian theology; it is through Augustine that T.F. Torrance reads the Eastern fathers.[234]

In contrast to Cyril of Alexandria

Torrance perceives an ontological priority to the "transcendent Trinity."[235] The main issue in Torrance's doctrine of the Holy Trinity is, when contrasted to Cyril, the ontological priority of the essence holds an exaggerated weight, where God's Being is to be found in his *ousia*. Cyril notes that God is "ontologically *hyperousios*," i.e. beyond essence.[236] Torrance speaks of the *ousia* as denoting Being in its *internal* relations.[237] *Ousia* for him is the *being* or the *identity*.[238] This is to be contrasted to the *hypostasis* as denoting the "being in its inter-personal objective relations" in the Holy Trinity, according to Torrance.[239] So, in a sense, this suggests that Torrance's *monarchia*—even if it is a *monarchia* of the whole Trinity—may seem Modalistic.

---

[233] Colin E. Gunton, *Father, Son and Holy Spirit*, 38.
[234] Ibid., 51.
[235] Nikolaos Asproulis, "T. F. Torrance and John Zizioulas on the Divine Monarchia: The Cappadocian Background and the Neo-Cappadocian Solution," 168.
[236] Russell, *Cyril of Alexandria*, 23.
[237] Colin E. Gunton, *Father, Son and Holy Spirit*, 48.
[238] Baker and Speidell, *T. F. Torrance and Eastern Orthodoxy*, 172.
[239] Thomas F. Torrance, *Trinitarian Perspectives: Toward Doctrinal Agreement* (London: A&C Black, 2000), 131.

The matter requires an extensive survey of Torrances' work and writings which is beyond the scope of this research, but it was important to here signal the corollary of their paradigm. Accordingly, Asproulis views "Torrance's definite distinction between the being and person of the Father could recall Modalistic connotations."[240] It seems that Torrance does not recognize the developments that took place concerning the term *hypostasis* beyond Athanasius.[241] As discussed earlier, this hypothesis subordinates *hypostasis* to *ousia*, hence, demoting the ontological priority of personhood. Torrance gives priority to the one being manifested in the one *ousia*.[242] This is further emphasized by Torrance's insistence on the Son's generation and the Spirit's procession from the Being of the Father rather than from His person. Concerning this latter point, Cyril stands in contrast as he asserted that the Son is the fruit of the Father's *hypostasis*.[243] Cyril's first writings, too, gave much attention to the Arian heresy—as appears in T.F. Torrance's writings—before turning later on to Nestorious. In this first phase of writing, Cyril illustrated his Trinitarian theology in *Dialogues on the Trinity*. Though Cyril of Alexandria used the term *"mia arche"*—which Torrance borrowed—refuting any subordination in the Holy Trinity, he maintains an ontological priority of personhood. The matter is proved true through his Christological

---

[240] Baker and Speidell, *T. F. Torrance and Eastern Orthodoxy*, 187.
[241] Ibid.
[242] Ibid., 172.
[243] Loon, *The Dyophysite Christology of Cyril of Alexandria*, 129.

writings as elucidated earlier. Likewise, T. F. Torrance opposes any causal relations in the Trinity and cites Cyril to refute the primacy of the Father, and Alan Torrance in turn takes the same position.[244] Cyril's perception of Trinitarian unity is founded on the coinherence of the persons and their *perichoretic* existence.[245] The Torrances' Trinitarian theology is well established in the doctrine of the persons but at the same time is safeguarding itself, with an eclipsing personified unity of being, against polytheism.

The Theology of John Zizioulas

In Contrast to the Ancient Catholic Church and Her Terminology

Zizioulas' Trinitarian theology seems to be solely dependent on the Cappadocian fathers.[246] Zizioulas is especially in appreciation for their development of the ontology of the person. But more specifically, he depends on Basil, where he promotes the latter's monarchy of the Father.[247] Zizioulas emphasizes the causal relations within the Holy Trinity. His doctrine of God features an

---

[244] Tingcui Jiang, "A Critical Study on Zizioulas' Ontology of Personhood" (Thesis, Hong Kong Baptist University, 2014), 14.
[245] Robert Isaac Wilberforce, *The Doctrine of the Incarnation of Our Lord Jesus Christ, in Its Relation to Mankind and to the Church* (London: John Murray, 1852), 143.
[246] Nikolaos Asproulis, "T. F. Torrance and John Zizioulas on the Divine Monarchia: The Cappadocian Background and the Neo-Cappadocian Solution," 165.
[247] Zizioulas, *Being as Communion*, 41.

ontological priority of personhood in contrast to essence, as per Asproulis.[248]

The most important terms employed in Zizioulas' Trinitarian theology are *ekstasis*, communion, and *hypostatic* union. The notion of *ekstasis* has Scriptural basis, but Zizioulas' understanding of it might stir some confusion. Does *ekstasis* comprise the termination of someone's entity in Zizioulas' paradigm?

In contrast to Cyril of Alexandria

John Zizioulas builds his whole theological argument on the ontology of personhood;[249] he may be called the "theologian of personhood." Nevertheless, Zizioulas holds an idiosyncratic ontology of personhood, that found no few opponents. He seems to build his understanding of the person on human and social relations.[250] Cyril, in contrast, derives his doctrine of God from the Divine revelation itself, handed to the Church and manifested in her tradition, saying:

> "Such is the true and upright teaching that the wisdom of the holy fathers has taught us: thus we have been trained also by the Holy Scriptures themselves to speak and to think."[251]

---

[248] Nikolaos Asproulis, "T. F. Torrance and John Zizioulas on the Divine Monarchia: The Cappadocian Background and the Neo-Cappadocian Solution," 167.
[249] Ibid., 166.
[250] Zizioulas, *Being as Communion*, 42,43.
[251] Cyril of Alexandria, *Commentary on John*, 2:265.

Zizioulas holds an ontological priority of personhood over the essence, as does Cyril of Alexandria. For Zizioulas, what a being *is* finds its answer in the person, his truthful reality or identity, where Zizioulas appoints the ontological principle in God to the person.[252] He opposes ancient Greek philosophy in that it connects God's unity and being to the substance (*ousia*), i.e. he refutes the ontological priority of the essence.[253] But the point at which Zizioulas diverges from Cyril of Alexandria is in confining God's *being* solely to the person of the Father.[254] Thus here explicitly, Zizioulas advocates a monarchy of the Father and consequently subordinates the Son and the Spirit to the Father. Cyril on the other hand, believes in a *mia arche* of the Holy Trinity.[255] The patriarch opposes any subordination within the Holy Trinity and is against any causal relations in the ontological Trinity.[256] Zizioulas makes use of the notion of *hypostatic* union—coined by Cyril of Alexandria—to further illustrate the ontological priority of personhood, contrasting the theological views of the West (represented by Pope Leo I) and that of the East (represented by Cyril of Alexandria).[257]

---

[252] Zizioulas, *Being as Communion*, 39.
[253] Ibid., 40.
[254] Ibid.
[255] Torrance, *Persons in Communion*, 294.
[256] Torrance, *Trinitarian Faith*, 338.
[257] Zizioulas, *Being as Communion*, 55.

Conclusion

Torrancean thought presents Trinitarian theology as being in line with the patristic doctrine of God. T.F. Torrance also supports his arguments with the Scriptures, and depends more on Athanasius and Cyril of Alexandria than on any other Church fathers. Nevertheless, the doctrine of the Torrances is still dominated by the Western emphasis of the one *ousia* (essence). This is an outcome of being occupied with safeguarding God's oneness. Ultimately the ontological priority of personhood is demoted being overshadowed by that of the essence.

Zizioulas identifies two different ways through which the unity or oneness of God is approached: first, is through the one and common essence (Augustinian and western approach) and second, is through the *monarchia* of the person of the Father (Cappadocian approach).[258]

To this, a third approach can be added: that of Cyril's (or the Alexandrian approach). Cyril, maintaining an ontological priority of personhood, recognizes the Divine oneness as being founded on the mutual indwelling of the Divine Persons and their coinherence, what can be called the perichoretic existence.[259] At the same time, Cyril opposes any causal relations in the Trinity,[260] while he

---

[258] Nikolaos Asproulis, "T. F. Torrance and John Zizioulas on the Divine Monarchia: The Cappadocian Background and the Neo-Cappadocian Solution," 174.
[259] Torrance, *Persons in Communion*, 294.
[260] Torrance, *Trinitarian Faith*, 338.

recognizes the commonly shared attributes of the *hypostases*, i.e. the notion of *homoousion*. Likewise, the patriarch does recognize the one *ousia* as what manifests the oneness of the Holy Trinity. Still, Cyril maintains the ontological priority of personhood grounded in the *hypostasis/prosopon*.

Ultimately Cyril's Trinitarian theology, manifested in his writings, can help resolve the modern theological debate taking place between the Torrances and John Zizioulas through fixing the shortcomings of each respectively.

Further Implications

On Christian Epistemology

Cyril's ontological priority of personhood can put the Christian epistemology on the right track. The knowledge of God is the knowledge of the Father who is revealed through the Son. Humanity is unable to gain knowledge of God except through personal participation in God's mode of existence. Once more, Cyril's doctrine of God is founded on the mutual indwelling of the persons and their coinherence. An example of this is found in Cyril's commentary on John 14:10.[261] The Son knows the Father fully through their natural union. In turn, how is humanity to know God? What are the main characteristics of Christian epistemology?

Firstly, Christian epistemology is ontological. Various philosophies throughout history failed to give a satisfactory answer to the ontological question of the material world.[262] The Orthodox concept of knowledge draws its principles from the truth that man realizes his being in God. Humanity's created being is hypostatized in God,[263] where it attains noetic self-awareness and the

---

[261] Cyril of Alexandria, *Commentary on John*.
[262] Christos Yannaras, *Orthodoxy and the West: Hellenic Self-Identity in the Modern Age* (Brookline: Holy Cross Orthodox Press, 2007), 26.
[263] Ibid.

knowledge of God. The intellectual knowledge is then the fruit of this ontological grasp (*ennoia*).[264]

Secondly, it is phenomenological. Knowledge in Orthodoxy is subjective rather than being objective, experiential rather than intellectual, as opposed to the Aristotelian ideology.[265] God is known through the *nous*— the eyes of the heart, or man's superior and inner conscious—as contrasted to the brain, an organ of the nervous system that collects data of the visible reality through the senses. The former yields transformation on the ontological level in man while the latter yields intellectual observations. The Church expresses her own experience through logical formulae, but this is not to replace the propinquity of the lived experience.[266]

Thirdly, it is personal. Orthodox theology has the Holy Trinity at its core. Gnosiology[267] in Orthodox understanding is acquired through communion with the hypostases: man knows the Son through the Spirit, and knows the Father through the Son and the Holy Spirit.[268] Knowledge is the fruit of being united to God. The faithful

---

[264] Daniel Buxhoeveden and Gayle Woloschak, *Science and the Eastern Orthodox Church* (Burlington: Ashgate Publishing, Ltd., 2013), 187.

[265] Allan M. Savage, *The Ecology: A "New to You" View: An Orthodox Theological Ecology* (Allan Savage, 2008), 35.

[266] Yannaras, *Orthodoxy and the West*, 25.

[267] Gnosiology can be compared to epistemology or 'how we know something'. This is usually thought of as an intellectual process. In the Christian context, Gnosiology addresses the knowledge of God particularly, and this, as discussed here, turns to be an ontological event.

[268] Vladimir Lossky, *In the Image and Likeness of God* (Yonkers: SVS Press, 1974), 16.

realizes his true *persona* through communion with the Holy Trinity, i.e. the true Persons. The Holy Trinity exists in a communion of love with reciprocal *ekstasis*. This is God's call to humanity, to participate in the Divine mode of existence, personal existence. A personal existence exceedingly transcends a natural existence limited by selfishness and necessities. Cyril of Alexandria commenting on: "if ye had known Me, ye would have known My Father also" (John 14:7), emphasizes that:

> "Christ seems to absolutely exclude those who hold this opinion (that it is needless to know the doctrine of the Trinity) from a true knowledge concerning God... For it is through the Son that we must draw near to God the Father."[269]

History repeats itself: the innovation of Sabellius (modalistic monarchianism) is reborn when modern theology presents God only as a monarchy to the faithful, demoting the *hypostases* to internal relations within the Divine essence.[270] The key point in developing the methodology of Orthodox theology and Christian epistemology is to reconsider the priority of the *Person*. This is nothing new, the theology of the Alexandrian Church—demonstrated in the writings of Cyril—has always maintained that the *hypostasis* is the cause and

---

[269] *Commentary on John*, 2:244.
[270] Yannaras, *Orthodoxy and the West*, 33.

maker of nature (essence).²⁷¹ In contrast, the priority of the essence mandates a specific stance towards epistemology, that is, reducing God to an object of thought.²⁷²

On Soteriology

Cyril's perspective of salvation, in a greater part of it, is dependent on the ontological becoming of man in Christ, founded on the Word's incarnational becoming. Through the mystical event of the Incarnation, human nature was *hypostatically* united to the person of the Word. The ontological priority of personhood, in Cyril's writings, helps to answer the question of how man can correctly receive salvation. In other words, what is the truthful message of salvation that the Church is proclaiming to the world?

> "It was not otherwise possible for man, being of a nature which perishes, to escape death, unless he recovered that ancient grace, and partook once more of God who holds all things together in being and preserves them in life through the Son in the Spirit. Therefore his Only-begotten Word has become a partaker of flesh and blood (Heb. 2: 14), that is, he has become man—though being Life by nature, and begotten of the

---

[271] John Ziziollas, *Al'wogood Sharika*, trans. St. Anthony Foundation, Second (Cairo, Egypt: St. Anthony Foundation, 2006), 98, translator's footnote.

[272] Yannaras, *Orthodoxy and the West*, 34.

Life that is by nature, that is, of God the Father—so that, having united himself with the flesh which perishes according to the law of its own nature, [...] he might restore it to his own life and render it through himself a partaker of God the Father [...] And he wears our nature, refashioning it to his own life. And he himself is also in us, for we have all become partakers of him, and have him in ourselves through the Spirit. For this reason we have become 'partakers of the divine nature' (2. Pet. 1:4), and are reckoned as sons, and so too have in ourselves the Father himself through the Son."[273]

In the last passage, salvation according to Cyril, is understood as participating in the eternal Trinitarian life through the *hypostatic* union that took place in the event of Incarnation. Thus, man participates in the Divine nature, i.e. divinized, where he actualizes his being through personal union with Christ. As a result, the perishing nature of man, by corruption, is healed (the literal meaning of *salved*), and death reigns no more. Accordingly, man acquires his true identity or reality (*physis*) through being united with the Holy Trinity. This is more emphasized through Cyril's dependence on 2 Peter 1:4 "γένησθε θείας κοινωνοὶ φύσεως," to explain God's salvation plan.[274]

---

[273] Cyril of Alexandria, *Commentary on John*, vol. 2, v. 14:20.
[274] Weinandy and Keating, *The Theology of St. Cyril of Alexandria*, 176.

In contrast to this Cyrillian concept is the ontological priority of the essence which, in turn, demotes the Divine persons, rendering them as mere Divine attributes. This is what appears in the theology of Paul of Samosata and Abū Rāi'ṭa Al-Takriti (illustrated earlier). The consequence of this deformed theology dangerously impacts the proclamation of Divine salvation. Evidently, the focus on the glory of the Divine essence and the beauty of the Divine attributes dominated preaching in most of the theological discourses. God is loving, good, mighty, truthful, faithful, and the list goes on. Though there is nothing wrong with this message, the problem is that it does not provide a means for humanity to participate in God's life. The only available route in those discourses, for humankind, is that of imitation. The faithful are receiving the wrong direction: solely practicing good morals. Christian theology becomes moralistic and Jesus Christ the Savior, in turn, becomes an exemplar, whose attributes are to be acquired through training. This is contrasted to how the Lord introduced his person as the door or the way for the knowledge of the person of the Father (Joh 14:6), where knowledge here means the fruit of being united to the person as illustrated earlier.

On Ecclesiology

In the first dialogue of his *Dialogues on the Trinity*, Cyril explains the triunity of God through the differentiation of the human hypostases which have in common the human essence. It is important, according to Cyril, to recognize the diversity within this unity. On the other hand, placing the notion of the one essence center stage overshadows the peculiarity and uniqueness of the persons. This can be perceived in Torrance's overemphasizing the homogeneity of the Being.

Arianism undermined the Divinity of Christ, reducing Him to a mediator. It was an attempt to preserve the oneness of God in a monarchic monotheism.[275] On the other hand, Sabellianism dissolved the Divinity of Christ in monarchical modalism.[276] Both were attempts to protect the unity of God at the expense of the true existence of distinct and coequal Divine persons.

The ontological priority of personhood as contrasted to that of the essence can be reflected in the realm of church life and ministry. The nascent Church of the New Testament had diversity as a fundamental characteristic from the very beginning.[277] This is evident in the incorporation of women in the ministry of the Church and, also, the grafting of the Gentiles into the body of Christ acknowledged in the multiplicity of tongues on the day of Pentecost. Within the Church, personal relationships become a parallel realm, accessible for those who are willing to participate in it. Attention must be given to the fact that the modalistic concept of Sabellius: when implemented in Church life,

---

[275] Moltmann, *The Trinity and the Kingdom*, 132.
[276] Ibid., 136.
[277] John M. Farrelly, *The Trinity: Rediscovering the Central Christian Mystery* (Lanham: Rowan & Littlefield Publishers, Inc., 2005), 263.

dissolves the personhood of the members.[278] Of course, all with the good intention of preserving unity.

In contrast, a theology as that of Rahner's—emphasizes the individualistic nature of God—will yield the regression of personal relations within the Church community.[279] The uniqueness of each member of the Church, along with his talents and role, is undermined. This uniqueness which is extant, only, in contrast to one who is another.

The sociality of the Holy Trinity, i.e. the *perichoretic* life, sets the relational pattern for the members of the Kingdom of God,[280] i.e. the Church. The Holy Trinity as the Divine society is both transcendent and revealed. Revealed through the prophetic activity of the Holy Spirit in the men of God, the Incarnation of the Son of God, and through the implanted natural human relationships. Therefore, studying the essential characteristics of social life can represent a reflection of the mode of existence of the Holy Trinity.[281] Contrastively, the revelation of the Holy Trinity can educate humans on how their lives can be transfigured.

Also, Monarchian theology has detrimental insinuations in the topic of Church inter-denominational relationships. A universal religion is the legitimate heir of

---

[278] Moltmann, *The Trinity and the Kingdom*, 136.
[279] Ibid., 146.
[280] Ibid., 198.
[281] Boff, *Trinity and Society*, 119.

monotheistic monarchianism.[282] When different Churches adopt monarchianism as their official perspective of God, a reflection of this is that they will demand dominance over each other. There will be no place for coexistence in love and communion. On the contrary, struggles breakout and ex-communications stand firm. The Churches' united diversity should be the sign needed that the world may believe.[283] The Church united in diversity is the verification of the truth of the Holy Trinity for the sake of the world's salvation.

---

[282] Moltmann, *The Trinity and the Kingdom*, 131.
[283] Ibid., 202.

Appendix

The Mystery of the Holy Trinity

by Andrei Rublev

1411 CE or 1425-1427 CE

The cover photo is of the famous Russian icon written by Andrei Rublev (died in the 15th century), titled *The Mystery of the Trinity*. A similar icon was initially used to illustrate *The Hospitality of Abraham*, but Rublev removed the figures of Abraham and Sarah to depict the Church's belief of the Holy Trinity.

The icon represents the scene from Genesis 18:1–8 illustrating the visitation of the three angels. Among the important characteristics of the scene, is the reciprocity of the Holy Trinity and coequality with the distinction of the three Persons, symbolized by different worn garments: The Father, the source, is depicted in gold garments on the left. Gold represents kingship. The Son is the middle figure, blessing the cup in the center, and donned in a blue garment which represents divinity. The Holy Spirit is seated on the right side, donned in green garments which symbolize new life. He points to the fourth seat at the table, inviting the viewer to communion with God (The Spirit […] say[s], 'Come!'" (Rev 22:17)). Also, it shows how the Holy Trinity lives in communion, signified by the commonly shared table. The inclined heads manifest the personal inclination of each Person towards the others as does the equal placement of the throne. The icon implements a reverse perspective, though it may look inartistic, that sets the focal point on the observer, as if the Trinity is spectating the observer, where the Holy Trinity owns the center of reality.

Bibliography

A Select Library of Nicene and Post-Nicene Fathers of the Christian Church. Edited by Philip Schaff and Henry Wace. 28 vols. in 2 series. 1886–1889. Repr., Grand Rapids: Wm. B. Eerdmans Publishing, 1987.

Baker, Matthew, and Todd H. Speidell. *T. F. Torrance and Eastern Orthodoxy: Theology in Reconciliation*. Eugene: Wipf and Stock Publishers, 2015.

Basil of Caesarea. *The Sacred Writings of Saint Basil*. Translated by Blomfield Jackson. Alternmünster: Jazzybee Verlag, 2012.

Behr, John. *The Nicene Faith*. Yonkers: SVS Press, 2004.

———. *The Way to Nicaea*. Yonkers: SVS Press, 2001.

Boff, Leonardo. *Trinity and Society*. Maryknoll: Orbis Books, 1988.

Bray, Gerald L. *We Believe in One God*. Downers Grove: IVP Academic, 2009.

Brouwer, Rinse H. Reeling. *Karl Barth and Post-Reformation Orthodoxy*. Burlington: Ashgate Publishing, Ltd., 2015.

Burris, Ronald D. *Where Is the Church?: Martyrdom, Persecution, and Baptism in North Africa from the Second to the Fifth Century*. Eugene: Wipf and Stock Publishers, 2012.

Buxhoeveden, Professor Daniel, and Professor Gayle Woloschak. *Science and the Eastern Orthodox Church*. Burlington: Ashgate Publishing, Ltd., 2013.

Colin E. Gunton. *Father, Son and Holy Spirit: Toward a Fully Trinitarian Theology*. London: T & T Clark International, 2003.

Colle, Ralph Del. "'Person' and 'Being' in John Zizioulas' Trinitarian Theology: Conversations with Thomas Torrance and Thomas Aquinas." *Scottish Journal of Theology* 54, no. 1 (February 2001): 70–86.

Cyril of Alexandria. *Commentary on John*. Translated by Members of the English Church. Vol. 2. London: W. Smith, 1885.

Dorner, Isaak August. *History of the Development of the Doctrine of the Person of Christ*. Edinburgh: T. & T. Clark, 1889.

Due, William J. La. *Trinity Guide to the Trinity*. London: A&C Black, 2003.

The Ecumenical Legacy of the Cappadocians. Edited by Dumitraşcu, Nicu. New York: Palgrave Macmillan, 2015.

Espín, Orlando O., and James B. Nickoloff. *An Introductory Dictionary of Theology and Religious Studies*. Collegeville: Liturgical Press, 2007.

Farrelly, John M. *The Trinity: Rediscovering the Central Christian Mystery*. Lanham: Rowman & Littlefield Publishers, Inc., 2005.

Fowler, James A. *Theo-Unity*. Fallbrook: Christ in You Publishing, 2008.

Giles, Kevin N. *Jesus and the Father: Modern Evangelicals Reinvent the Doctrine of the Trinity*. Grand Rapids: Zondervan Academic, 2009.

González, Justo L. *A History of Christian Thought: From the Beginnings to the Council of Chalcedon*. Nashville: Abingdon Press, 1987.

Gunton, Colin. "Trinitarian Perspectives. Towards Doctrinal Agreement. By Thomas F. Torrance. Edinburgh: T&T Clark, 1994. Pp. 149. £18.95." *Scottish Journal of Theology* 52, no. 3 (August 1999): 379–80.

Harnack, Adolf. *History of Dogma*. Vol. 1. Eugene: Wipf and Stock Publishers, 1997.

Hillar, Marian. *From Logos to Trinity: The Evolution of Religious Beliefs from Pythagoras to Tertullian*. Cambridge: Cambridge University Press, 2012.

Jiang, Tingcui. "A Critical Study on Zizioulas' Ontology of Personhood." Thesis, Hong Kong Baptist University, 2014. https://repository.hkbu.edu.hk/etd_oa/108?utm_source=repository.hkbu.edu.hk%2Fetd_oa%2F108&utm_medium=PDF&utm_campaign=PDFCoverPages.

Kärkkäinen, Veli-Matti. *The Trinity: Global Perspectives*. Louisville: Presbyterian Publishing Corporation, 2007.

Kasper, Walter. *Jesus the Christ: New Edition*. London: A&C Black, 2011.

Loon, Hans van. *The Dyophysite Christology of Cyril of Alexandria*. Leiden: Brill, 2009.

Lossky, Vladimir. *In the Image and Likeness of God*. Yonkers: SVS Press, 1974.

Martyr, Justin. *The Sacred Writings of Justin Martyr*. Alternmünster: Jazzybee Verlag, 2012.

McCall, Thomas. *Which Trinity? Whose Monotheism? Philosophical and Systematic Theologians on the Metaphysics of Trinitarian Theology*. Grand Rapids: Wm. B. Eerdmans Publishing, 2010.

McGuckin, John. *St. Cyril of Alexandria: The Christological Controversy: Its History, Theology, and Texts*. Leiden: Brill, 1994.

Moltmann, Jurgen. *The Trinity and the Kingdom*. Minneapolis: Fortress Press, 1993.

Nikolaos Asproulis. "T. F. Torrance and John Zizioulas on the Divine Monarchia: The Cappadocian Background and the Neo-Cappadocian Solution." *Participatio: Journal of the Thomas F. Torrance Theological Fellowship* 4 (2013).

Olson, Roger E. *The Story of Christian Theology: Twenty Centuries of Tradition Reform*. Downers Grove: IVP Academic, 1999.

Olson, Roger E., and Christopher Alan Hall. *The Trinity*. Grand Rapids: Wm. B. Eerdmans Publishing, 2002.

Peters, Ted. *God as Trinity: Relationality and Temporality in Divine Life*. Louisville: Westminster John Knox Press, 1993.

Ramelli, Ilaria. "Origen's Anti-Subordinationism and Its Heritage in the Nicene and Cappadocian Line." *Vigiliae Christianae* 65, no. 1 (January 1, 2011): 21–49.

———. *The Christian Doctrine of Apokatastasis: A Critical Assessment from the New Testament to Eriugena*. Leiden: Brill, LL2013.

Rausch, Thomas P. *Who Is Jesus? An Introduction to Christology*. Collegeville: Liturgical Press, 2003.

Rogers, Rick. *Theophilus of Antioch: The Life and Thought of a Second-Century Bishop*. Lanham: Lexington Books, 2000.

Russell, Norman. *Cyril of Alexandria*. London: Routledge, 2000.

Savage, Allan M. *The Ecology: A "New to You" View: An Orthodox Theological Ecology*. Allan Savage, 2008.

Select Treatises of S. Athanasius, Archbishop of Alexandria in Controversy with the Arians in *A Library of Fathers of the Holy Catholic Church Anterior to the Division of the East and West*. London: Rivington, 1844.

Shepherd, Victor A. "Thomas F. Torrance and the Homoousion of the Holy Spirit." *Participatio: Journal of the Thomas F. Torrance Theological Fellowship* 3 (2012).

Tertullian. *The Writings of Tertullian - Volume I Revised*. Lulu.com, n.d.

The Faith of the Early Fathers: Pre-Nicene and Nicene Eras. Translated by William A. Jurgens. Collegeville: Liturgical Press, 1970.

Toom, Tarmo. *Classical Trinitarian Theology: A Textbook*. New York: Bloomsbury Publishing, 2007.

Torrance, Alan. *Persons in Communion: Trinitarian Description and Human Participation*. London: A&C Black, 1996.

Torrance, Thomas F. *Divine Meaning: Studies in Patristic Hermeneutics*. London: T&T Clark, 1995.

———. *Theological and Natural Science*. Eugene: Wipf and Stock, 2005.

———. *Trinitarian Faith: The Evangelical Theology of the Ancient Catholic Faith*. Edition Unstated edition. London: T&T Clark, 2000.

———. *Trinitarian Perspectives: Toward Doctrinal Agreement*. London: A&C Black, 2000.

Volf, Miroslav. *After Our Likeness: The Church as the Image of the Trinity*. Grand Rapids: Wm. B. Eerdmans Publishing, 1998.

Webster, John. *The Cambridge Companion to Karl Barth*. Cambridge: Cambridge University Press, 2000.

Weinandy, Thomas, and Daniel A. Keating. *The Theology of St. Cyril of Alexandria: A Critical Appreciation*. London: A&C Black, 2003.

Wilberforce, Robert Isaac. *The Doctrine of the Incarnation of Our Lord Jesus Christ, in Its Relation to Mankind and to the Church*. London: John Murray, 1852.

Williams, Rowan. *Arius: Heresy and Tradition*. Norwich: SCM Press, 2001.

Yannaras, Christos. *Orthodoxy and the West: Hellenic Self-Identity in the Modern Age.* Brookline: Holy Cross Orthodox Press, 2007.

———. *Relational Ontology.* Edited by Norman Russell. Brookline: Holy Cross Orthodox Press, 2011.

Zizioulas, John D. *Al'wogood Sharika.* Translated by St. Anthony Foundation. Cairo: St. Anthony Foundation, 2006.

———. *Being as Communion: Studies in Personhood and the Church.* Yonkers: SVS Press, 1985.

———. *Communion and Otherness: Further Studies in Personhood and the Church.* New York: Bloomsbury Publishing, 2010.

———. "Human Capacity and Human Incapacity: A Theological Exploration of Personhood1." *Scottish Journal of Theology* 28, no. 5 (October 1975): 401–47. doi:10.1017/S003693060003533X.

About the Author

Sherif Mourad is an ordained Reader (Anagnostes) in the Coptic Orthodox Church. He is the president of al-Tareek Coptic Foundation for Christian Studies and Orthodox Spirituality, which he founded in 2013 and a lecturer at Holy Transfiguration College, Agora University, USA. Sherif holds a Master of Theology from Agora University. His research focuses on Systematic Theology (Orthodox Dogmatics, Coptic Orthodox Christology, and Soteriology), Patristic Studies (especially Cyril of Alexandria), Biblical Theology, and Orthodox Spirituality. He is also a translator of a number of books on Orthodox spirituality. As a licensed pharmacist in Egypt, Sherif has been running his private pharmacy since 2005.

www.ingramcontent.com/pod-product-compliance
Lightning Source LLC
Chambersburg PA
CBHW030532080526
44586CB00011B/400